Every Contractor's Selling Handbook:

How To Round Up Prospects,

Build Value, and Get Referrals

By: Justin C. Jones

Published by Justin C. Jones
Clearwater, FL 33761

ISBN-13: 9780615868837
ISBN-10: 0615868835

Printed in the United States of America
DISCLAIMER AND/OR LEGAL NOTICES

Table of Contents:

Introduction

What business are we really in? Well, we *DO* contracting, but in order to get on location and start the job, we must first *SELL* our contracting services to individuals and businesses. Whether we like it or not, we have to reach out to people. Without prospective customers, we can't do what we love to do. So, when I am asked what business I am in, my answer is always, "I am in the *People Business.*"

As I see it, because I am a contractor, people are my first priority. My job is to:

1. Locate people who need my services

2. Use key questions to understand exactly what they need done

3. Demonstrate "value"—how I can do this job better than the next guy

4. Develop a pleasant, working relationship with them that carries us through the contracting job

5. Maintain that relationship so that I can get referrals for other clients from them

<u>This handbook will demonstrate exactly how to accomplish this and how you can succeed as a contractor.</u>

Most contractors can describe what they do, but "selling" your business to your potential client involves more than just talking about what you do. Your ability to set up a meeting, build value, and ultimately leave with a contract depends on your ability to "sell yourself." *YOU* have to come across as honest, dependable, and caring so your prospect immediately trusts you as a person. At the same time, you have to present your expertise and experience in such a way that your prospect also trusts that you are capable of doing the job right.

Most contractors are put at a disadvantage when it comes to presenting and "selling" our business to prospective customers. When we study for our contracting license, we are not taught how to "sell ourselves." There is nothing—ZERO—in the textbooks about selling, customer service, follow-up, and how to find prospective customers. The contracting exam consists mostly of technical and practical knowledge, and perhaps some general business facts, but contractors have been left high and dry with no clue how to bring in new business.

In this handbook, we will cover key elements of selling from prospecting for the right clients to establishing your value (what separates you from the competition), to polishing your presentation, to getting great referrals. These elements will not only jumpstart your business, but they will keep your business thriving, despite the tough economy.

Whether you specialize in electrical, plumbing, roofing, painting, flooring, or general contracting, you exhibit your expertise in everything you do.

However, all of your training and experience is useless, unless you can also bring in new clients. This is the hard part. You have spent your life perfecting your craft. How are you supposed to suddenly become an expert in sales and marketing when running your business takes up all your time and energy?

Over the past 10 years, sales and marketing methods have shifted. A decade ago, you could run an ad in the Yellow Pages and your local paper, and the phone would ring. If your ad was bigger, your phone would ring more. Work was abundant. We were automatically considered the expert in our fields. All we had to do was show up, write an estimate, and schedule the work right there.

Times have drastically changed. Now, potential customers go through their own screening processes before ever selecting a contractor. The days of opening the Yellow Pages and making calls are extinct.

Today's consumer will actively research online before calling you or anyone. By the time the customer calls, he has already researched possible solutions for his problem, checked out numerous contractors in the area, and tapped into social media for customer reviews and recommendations. The consumer has already narrowed down his list of contractors and has viewed contractors' websites to get a feel for their companies. As a result, consumers know far more about you than you know about them. No longer can you just post an ad. Now, you must stand out from your competitors and prove to particular prospects why they should trust you.

<u>This is where I can help</u>. I am a contractor, and have been for 13 years. I was fortunate enough to pick up valuable sales and marketing skills along the way. This handbook shares those skills with you in the following chapters, so you can gain expertise in marketing your own contracting business to potential customers.

With my easy-to-follow, step-by-step process, you will discover how to market yourself and your contracting business without losing precious time from working, studying, or taking courses.

Just implement my techniques in this handbook, and before you realize it, you will know the best way to approach a potential client—what to say, what NOT to say—and how to present your business in a way that will make that prospect eager to hire you. In this handbook, you will learn techniques for locating new prospects, showcasing your company's strengths, highlighting key features and benefits to the client, balancing value against cost, and effectively closing the sale. Moreover, you will discover how to turn your contracting company into a self-perpetuating business, where your happy customers refer you new customers.

Without these skills, your company will flounder against the competition. You need to know powerful ways to prove why and how your company will do the job better than the others, even if they try to undercut you on price. With this handbook, you will master how to increase the value of your contracting company in your prospects' minds and get them to sign the contract.

Acknowledgments: People I would like to take the time to thank:

My Lord and Savior for the Grace He has given me.

My lovely and talented wife Lily, and beautiful children Justin and Gianna. My dad, and two mothers.

My mentors: Jerry Freeman, for believing in me when not a lot of people did and Arry Housh, for taking me under your wing and showing me leadership and how to run a business while maintaining your faith.

Jinni, Tracy, and Stephanie for editing my words so everyone can read them.

Lastly, my fellow contractors whom I have worked with and loved over the years and who inspired this book.

ch: 1

Prospecting for Customers:

Where Do I Start?

Introduction:

This is one of the hardest questions to answer. When prospecting, you can cast a wide net and aim for everyone in a geographical region, or you can focus your efforts and reach a more targeted demographic. General prospecting reaches more people, but a fair number may not be particularly interested. Focused prospecting reaches a higher percentage of interested prospects, but if your scope is too narrow, you might prematurely rule out potential prospects. It is a constant balance.

Defining your target market

These questions must be answered to define your target market. Start with a description of your target market. Does your ideal client own a home? Is your target client within a certain income level? Who is your ideal client? Asking yourself these questions will help paint a picture of your ideal client. The next several chapters will go into finding your ideal client. The RAC method is a good starting point.

I use the **"RAC"** <u>Prospecting Method</u> for Residential and Commercial prospecting. Here it is in a nutshell:

<u>R-Research:</u>

All prospecting should start with research. You need to understand the "demographics" and the "psychographics" of the people you will be marketing to <u>before</u> trying to sell them anything.

<u>Demographics</u> provide critical facts you need to know about home or business owners in a set area. Demographics include information regarding education level, income, marital status, and housing. If you are a contractor, as I am, the information in which you will be specifically interested is the age of the home, if it is owner-occupied or rented, the number of bedrooms, and the size of the family. I have found the two best sources for these demographics are the U.S. Census Bureau website for 2012 (www.census.gov/compendia/statab/) and www.Movoto.com.

<u>Psychographics</u>, the second body of information you need, is the study of individuals and their communities—their likes and dislikes, spending habits, community involvement, and hobbies. You can access this type of information on social media websites and by doing Google searches for psychographics for the specific geographical areas in which you are interested. You can also check out specific businesses or brand names in that area and read the related testimonials. When you go to LinkedIn and Facebook pages of specific businesses and individuals, for example, you can read opinions customers/friends share on these sites, comments they make about particular products and services, responses to community issues, politics, and specific interests they have. This will give you a feel for what is important to people in

your target demographic. Knowing what makes them excited, happy, frustrated, or annoyed will allow you to present your product or service in a way that solves their problems.

By including both demographics and psychographics in your research, you have a greater chance of locating prospects who are most likely to become your new customers.

A-Avenue:

What avenues can you use to locate potential prospects in these communities? The answer is determining what their involvement is in their community. Use the following avenues to meet and talk with business owners, parents, employees, and community leaders:

Most communities have both professional and leisure <u>Associations</u>. Professional Associations range from medical, legal, and financial to specific trades. Some associations are linked to sports, schools, vocations, religions, or charities. Visit their websites to see whether their interests fit with what you are trying to promote. To be allowed to see all the pages of certain association websites, you may have to register and become a member.

<u>Organizations</u> are also a great place to prospect for potential customers. The local Chamber of Commerce puts you in touch with the businesses in each community. Again, you may have to become a member to see the business contact names, phone numbers, and email addresses. Non-profits like educational and religious organizations, as well as service organizations like the Rotary Club, all reveal where the heart and soul of any community is. Here you will discover what is deeply important to the residents of the municipality or county.

<u>Networking</u> is a third powerful avenue for you to locate potential prospects. Get plugged into the community you are targeting and find out where and when community and charity events and

networking socials are taking place. At these events you will have numerous opportunities to market your business, find out who the decision-makers are in the companies you are targeting, and spread goodwill.

C-Connect:

When contacting these organizations and individuals, what do you say? What is the best way to connect with them?

Connecting with people is a two-way street. You reach out to a prospect, and in return, that person responds back. You want the prospect's response to be positive and enthusiastic, so you must reach out with a positive attitude and enthusiasm. Your attitude, tone of voice, body language, message and trustworthiness all work together to create a reciprocal response from your prospect.

Before you meet your prospect in person, you need to lay the groundwork for that encounter. Introduce yourself and your business by sending an email or making a phone call as your first contact. When you show up at an event, you will already have made personal contact with a staff person. Sign up for networking events and bring along business cards and/or brochures displaying what your company does. Pass them out as you greet prospects. Also, collect as many business cards, phone numbers, and email addresses as possible.

Very few people can effectively make impromptu presentations, so take the time to formulate your introduction. Draft one presentation to be used as your phone introduction and another presentation memorized for in-person meetings. Also, prepare a written introduction for emails you send.

In your introduction, be sure to include answers to the following questions: What value can you offer the prospect? How are your products or installation better than the competitors'? Any questions you receive regularly should also be answered in your introduction.

I have created a spreadsheet that will help you develop your own plan for connecting with potential customers. I have also included key points that every contractor should use to spice up his Introduction so his business stands out from the competition. Once you have these tools in place, you can start enjoying prospecting for new customers. Don't wait, get started today. Good Prospecting!

My PRO Story

Soon after I first launched my contracting business, a buddy of mine, another contractor, told me that I must try networking. He invited me to attend a networking group, going on and on about how much it boosted his own business. I was a little reluctant, because I couldn't see what good it would do, but he insisted, saying, "You will meet business owners and other people who can send jobs your way. The meeting is free. What do you have to lose? Plus, you get lunch just for showing up." I was in once he mentioned "FREE" and "LUNCH." He gave me the address and told me to bring my business cards.

I showed up straight from a jobsite - dirty, covered with drywall dust. I looked around. There were 22 people in this group who met at a local buffet. During introductions, I had an opportunity to talk a little about myself and my business. I stood up and said my piece for about two minutes. I was shaking like a leaf and kept tripping over my own words. It was awful, but I got through it.

The next month when I showed up again, I made sure I had enough time to clean up first. I figured it was more important to look professional than to look like a hard worker. I was surprised, because this time the group took me more seriously. One member of the group was a realtor. After the meeting, he pulled me aside and suggested I check out "PRO," the local realtor organization. He didn't have a number or even an address. He kind of knew where it was located, but was not sure, so I resorted to my tried-and-true **RAC Method** to track it down:

(R) Research: I turned to my best friend Google and looked up where I needed to go. I also did a little digging to find out more information about the organization and what it did. I even checked out the organization's Facebook page and found several groups associated with PRO. One in particular stood out to me—the "Young Professional Group." I clicked on a link to that group, got all the information and found out who was in the group. The Young Professional Group met the third Wednesday of each month around lunchtime.

(A) Avenue: I showed up at this meeting dressed to impress, already knowing the names of some of the members in attendance. There were 16 people at the meeting: 12 realtors, two "PRO" employees, and two affiliates with mortgage broker and staging companies.

(C) Connect: Once inside, I walked around and talked with everyone, getting their contact information and sharing my business cards. When I got home after the meeting, I sent them each a "thank you" note. I made it a point to get to know them better over the next few weeks and even became involved in projects through PRO. I received my first lead after about two weeks from one of the realtors in the group. When I met with her on the jobsite, she told me about orientations that were available to realtors. At these realtor orientations, contracting companies were sometimes allowed to give five-minute presentations. She suggested that I go and participate.

I looked up the time and date for the next orientation and came prepared to briefly present my business—what products and services I offer and how I could help new realtors. Best of all, this was FREE exposure. I collected business cards and email addresses. I have since repeated this orientation process about 15 times and built a database of several hundred realtors I keep in touch with. One of the original 16 members of the group became the president of PRO, and I ended up handling several projects on PRO's building. I also received free advertising, because other realtors saw my signs while I was working on the PRO's building.

To date, I have several hundred realtor contacts, inspectors, and mortgage brokers who send me business because of my affiliation with PRO.

This is the **RAC Method** in action. Share your own story with me by emailing it to: Justin@ContractorsNetworking.com

ch 2:

Effectively Contacting your Prospects

With today's technology, you have a number of powerful ways to reach out to potential customers. Besides making contact in person and by line and mobile phone, you can also connect with future clients by email, text message, and social media. Here are some guidelines for using these methods effectively:

<u>Here is the method for non-referral-based prospects</u>

Suppose that last week you cold-called several local prospects and in-troduced yourself and your business, but you were unable to set up appointments because you could not get through to a decision-maker. What do you do now? Should you try going back in person another day to get that appointment? Would it be better to call or email the prospect and request a meeting, or should you wait a couple more days so that you do not appear too anxious? What about mailing your company's brochure or even doing an email campaign to get their attention? When you *do* finally reach the prospective business owner, what on earth do you say to convince him to hire you?

When cold-calling, if you speak to the business owner, make sure you ask how he (or she) prefers to be contacted—by phone, email, cell phone, or text message. Let him know you are aware of how busy he is and that you want to communicate in the way most convenient for him. Get the owner's direct or cell phone number and email address, if possible.

If you are only allowed to speak with the receptionist or assistant, still push for this vital information. You need a direct link to prospective business owners. If you are stonewalled by the "gatekeeper," leave your business card and a brochure, if you have one. Make sure that your website URL and your email address are on your marketing materials. If you have a business Facebook or LinkedIn page, put that URL on your card as well. This is another way to capture the curiosity of the business owner and get him to contact you.

Email and text messages are practical ways to contact prospects for several reasons:

(i) When you send an email or text message, you can reach your prospects 24/7 whether or not they are available at the moment;

(ii) Your message is in writing, so there are fewer chances there will be mistakes or confusion over details;

(iii) Moreover, you can send the emails or text messages at your own convenience, even when you are away from your office.

Cell phones may be the preferred means of communication for some prospects, because most people carry their cell phones with them. Potential customers may ask to be contacted by cell or mobile phone. This will work in your favor. Often trying to reach prospects on their office phones can be frustrating, especially if they are rarely in their offices and must be tracked down by the receptionist or by whoever happens to answer the phone when you call. With the cell phone, however, the person picking up is usually the cell phone owner and the person you are trying to reach.

Social Media sources, particularly Facebook, LinkedIn, and Twitter, have become popular ways for businesses to reach new prospects. These sources allow you to broadcast who and what your company is and what you do for your customers. They are also cost-effective for sharing coupons and specials that get the prospect to test out your products and services. Press releases and blogs can be posted on your Facebook page to get future customers reading about you and your company. Facebook, LinkedIn, Google+, and Twitter are "social," meaning lots of people see what you are sharing and can comment and respond. Great for advertising your business, they can also be used to prompt potential clients to tell you what they are looking for in a project. This critical information will help you gauge the market and fine-tune your marketing presentations.

When it comes to developing a personalized, one-on-one relationship with a potential customer, you need to tune out the rest of the world and focus only on that one client. You need to be specific. What you say to this client may differ from what you offer another customer, because customers' needs are different. Use various social media sources to advertise your business in creative ways and to reach large audiences, but use personalized methods like email, text messages, phone and, of course, face-to-face meetings to develop relationships with each customer.

How to Effectively Text your Prospects

When your potential client asks you to text him the information on his cell phone, it is best to follow the "less is more" rule. In other words, say what you have to say in as few words as possible. This will be far more effective than long, detailed paragraphs. Do not write a book when you text. Make it "short, sweet, and to the point." Only include what is necessary to that one communication, or you will lose your prospect in a sea of words. Text only bare bones - just enough to get him interested - and ask him to call or email you for the rest of the details, or to watch for your email with the critical documents attached.

Effectively Emailing Your Prospects

If you are emailing potential clients whom you have never met, write an attention-grabbing subject line and make the body of the email relevant, informative, and enjoyable to read. You can always attach brochures, details, charts, and spreadsheets.

When part of an ongoing email campaign, you can add color and pizzazz to your emails and set them up in a series. Design each email to provide some content and also to spark curiosity so your recipient is eager to read your next email. This helps coax the prospect to eventually come on board.

If you have already made a cold-call, your email becomes a serious relationship-building tool. The purpose of the email is to set up an appointment with your prospect or get an immediate answer from him, so keep your email message short and clear. Ask specific questions. Avoid using sentences that can be misconstrued or misunderstood. Attach additional information, such as a proposal or a copy of your newsletter that has related information.

It is best if you send your emails one at a time, unless you are advertising your business. If you send your message to dozens of email addresses at the same time, your email could get caught in the recipients' spam folders. Worse yet, you could be reported for spamming. To avoid this, use the BCC (Blind Carbon Copy) option if you must send the same email to several people. This feature displays your email recipient's own email address at the top and not all the other people to whom you sent the same email.

Also be careful to write a subject line that cannot be perceived as spam. For example, do not make your subject line say, "Friend, Here's a Great Deal from ….." Instead, whenever possible, be specific to that individual and write a subject line like, "Contracting Details per our Conversation."

Save Time by Using the Same Basic Script

Prepare yourself before sending an email, text message, or before you make a phone call. You only have a few seconds to catch the attention of business owners before they delete the message or hang up. Do not rely on your quick wit to convey your crucial message. Instead, adapt your in-person presentation to whichever medium you are using to contact your prospect. If you already have a phone script, adjust it further to fit whatever you are specifically talking about in your email, text message, or phone call. WRITE IT OUT BEFORE YOU USE IT. Do not assume that you can just "wing it" because chances are you will forget something important and have to re-contact the prospect to add the detail you forgot—not a very professional impression to leave.

Phone Call Preparation

Write down exactly what you plan to say in your phone call. Then, edit it down to the bare bones. Aim for 30 seconds or less. Add a catchy beginning to prick the prospect's curiosity and make him want to find out more about what you and your company can do. Your phone script should include your full name, purpose for the call, your phone number and the best time for the prospect to return your call.

Now practice this phone script until you are comfortable with the wording and know where to emphasize for the greatest impact. (You can also use this revised version as the basis for your voicemail messages, emails and text messages.)

When you call, do not be thrown off your game if your prospect tells you that he cannot talk right now. Respond by saying, "I just need 30 seconds (or a minute) to let you know what this is about." If he says okay, recite your planned script. Then offer to come by when it is more convenient to see how the relationship can be a good fit.

Give him an either or choice, "Would you prefer to meet on Thursday or Friday morning?" (For example) then negotiate the day and time with the prospect. This is much more effective than an open-ended question like, "So, when would you like to meet?"

If your prospect is not available when you call, have a <u>voicemail message</u> already prepared so you will sound professional when you leave your voicemail. The response you get from a rehearsed, well-written message will be far more positive than one that is hap-hazardly thrown together on the spot. Just like your phone script, your voice-mail must include your full name, purpose for the call, your phone number and the best time for the prospect to return your call.

The following will help you make the most out of the precious seconds while you have your prospect's ear. If you have a Bluetooth or headset on your phone, use it instead of the phone receiver. This will free up both your hands and your body while you talk. Most people are expressive with their hands and move their bodies when they talk in person. A phone call should be no different. Go ahead and be expressive while you talk on the phone. Be as descriptive and emphatic with your hands as you would be in person. Even stand up and walk around as you talk on the phone. Your energy and enthusiasm will be carried through your words. Believe it or not, relaxing and using your own body language will make you more effective and convincing to your prospect. This is how you get your prospect excited about your services. Hands-free phone calling will also make taking notes easier.

Putting your call on speaker phone is <u>not</u> a good substitute for the headset or Bluetooth, because the speaker phone echoes and makes your voice sound distant and uncaring. Plus, the prospect may be hesitant to talk openly with you if he thinks he might be overheard by others in the room. You want your call to be as personal as possible. You are trying to build trust. Do not sabotage yourself by using the speaker phone.

Making a Great First Impression

First impressions are critical for business success. Two key elements for making a powerful first impression are: 1. Be prepared and 2. Make an emotional connection with your prospect. As we discussed earlier, writing down and practicing your presentation for fluidity and emphasis—whether it is your cold-call, a phone call, or voicemail—is critical to making a great first impression. A well put-together email or text message will also ensure a great first impression. You must project your expertise and confidence in what you have to offer. At the same time, you have to engage the prospect emotionally; find out what he needs, and show how your company can meet those needs. The best way to do this is for you to be enthusiastic about how you can help the prospect's company.

As you talk with your prospect, make a point to use his name several times. This creates an unspoken bond between the two of you that supports an emotional connection. Be careful, however, not to be "salesy." Most people resent being cornered by a pushy salesman. Keep your presentation conversational, not pressuring. Your goal is to get your prospect to voluntarily share his business needs, not desperately search for a reason to get away from you.

Some contractors fall into the habit of "talking shop" with their prospects. A little of this may be helpful in getting your prospect to relax and to feel that you know what you are talking about, but do not get carried away. Talking shop can be distracting, time-consuming and, if you never quite get to talking about what you can do for the prospect, you will have wasted his time and lost the chance to close the deal. Stick to your planned presentation as closely as possible. That goes for in-person meetings as well as phone calls, emails and text messages. Your prospects are very busy people, and the second they feel you are tying up their time, they will refuse to do business with you.

Finally, know when to "shut up." This technique is true for all kinds of sales. After you have made your presentation, stop talking and give your prospective client a few moments to assimilate what you have said. If you keep repeating your points, you will end up coming across as desperate. Be confident in your presentation. Wait a bit and see if the prospect has any immediate questions. Answer them, then ask the prospect which parts of what you talked about made the most sense for the project. What seemed to fit his vision the best? Once your prospect expresses his opinion, see if you can match up specific services you can offer to what he is looking for. The more similarities, the more likely he will hire you for the job—because there will not be any reasons left not to. You will have answered all the prospect's concerns and swept away all his objections.

The Rory Vaden Story: Contacting

I was at a trade show in 2011 featuring Rory Vaden. He was explaining his story about trying to get in touch with publishers to look at his book manuscript. He explained how he would call and leave a message, but would never get a call back. Several times he would show up at a publisher's office and wander around, hoping to snag the attention of a publisher, but this did not work either. He was about to give up when the receptionist told him for the 39th time to send her a Facebook message. It seemed like a longshot, but he thought, "What the heck?" He got onto his computer and messaged the gatekeeper on Facebook. Within minutes his request was answered and a friend request popped into his inbox. He finally made his contact and was now in the loop. This contact led to getting his book published. You never know what type of contact method your potential client prefers, so do not be afraid to try different avenues until you get through.

Personally, I cannot stand texting; I think it is the evil stepchild of email. Short, annoying, and designed for teenagers who cannot communicate. I can't figure out why it is so popular. But, here is the thing that startled me cold. I discovered that my typical customers, who are in their late 40s and 50s, are starting to text me about jobs and send me their contact information via text messages. I have to respond and—trust me—I am brief. I finally asked one of these couples, "Why do you text me?" They answered, "Our children text us about everything. We just find it easier to text than to call." Their teenagers had gotten them into using text messages, and now they cannot stop. I immediately downloaded Evernote to organize my text messages and now send out about 30 text messages per day to potential customers. You know, it is really an effective way to communicate. The reason I have them crafted already is to save time and make sure my tone stays consistent.

ch 3:

Qualifying Prospects

Although it seems logical to try to convert every single prospect into a client for your company, it is actually more profitable and practical to screen or qualify them before pitching your products and services to them. "Qualifying" enables you to weed out potential clients that would end up being a poor fit and costing you extra time and money in the long run.

In order to qualify a prospect, you need to have a <u>pre-planned set of open-ended questions</u> to ask them. This is your <u>checklist</u>. These questions allow you to get a feel for the proposed project; the prospect's expectations for you; and what materials, specs and timeline he requires.

Run through your checklist with each prospect whether you are on the phone or in person. This way you will be able to ensure you have covered every critical aspect of the potential job. This checklist will also show you at a glance which prospects will be a great fit and which ones will probably bring issues and baggage into the negotiations. Every prospect who has unreasonable requirements or expectations will cost you time and dig into your profit margin. With the checklist, however, you will be able to weigh negatives against positives to determine if, despite your having to make a few accommodations, a prospect might end up being worth extra work on your part.

Your Checklist:

Contact Information:

The first section of your checklist will be the same for most prospects. You need to jot down their company name, owner's name, project manager's name (if different from the owner), the address of the company, the address of the project site, the main phone numbers, cell phone numbers, and email addresses of your contacts.

It is absolutely critical that you find out who the <u>decision-maker</u> is. If you are working with the project manager, but the general manager or owner is the person who makes the final decisions for the project, you can talk until you are blue in the face to the project manager and the information may not be approved by the decision-maker. In fact, details can easily be mixed up as they pass up the grapevine to the owner, and, like the game Whisper Down the Lane, some critical facts may never reach the person who does the final signing off. *GET THE NAME AND CONTACT INFORMATION OF THE DECISION-MAKER <u>NOW</u>*, while you are gathering the initial information on your checklist. If the decision-maker is not the person you are talking with and is not available to meet with you right now, thank the person you have been talking with and ask if you can set up an appointment with the decision-maker. Then come back and give your presentation to the right person. Otherwise, you will have to go through your entire presentation a second time.

One other note: As you gather information, <u>double check that there is only one decision maker</u>. Many companies have two or more people authorized to sign off on contracts. The second person could be a co-owner, silent partner, accountant, or even an attorney. You may need to meet with both the owner and the project manager. Make sure that you set up a meeting with all principal people involved in the project present.

Project Details:

Next on your checklist is the project itself. Now you can zero in on some of the specifics of the project. Encourage your prospect to explain the purpose of the project, the timeline, or schedule for various aspects of the project—including both construction and financial deadlines. Ask about the prospect's flexibility and let him know your flexibility and other deadlines. Get an overview of the size of the project, how much manpower and the type of equipment that will be needed, and see if you can get a peek at some of the specs so you can estimate the quality and price of the materials needed. This is "information-gathering." You are not committing to anything yet. Show your enthusiasm, but until you have a solid idea of the prospect's expectations and what is involved in the project, just keep nodding and taking notes. Most of all, continue asking key questions from your checklist to keep the prospect on topic.

Focus on things that are important to your prospect, but do not lose track of the things important to your own business. Keep a healthy balance between pleasing your prospect and doing things you know work for your company. The best way to do this is to make sure you understand "why" certain things are critical to the decision-maker. You find this out by asking him open-ended questions. Again, as you are discussing these details, also remember "why" you maintain certain standards and protocols. Communicate them to the prospect. Do not give up your standards just to make the sale - you will regret it later. Instead, negotiate with the prospect until you reach a delicate balance between what is important to your prospect and what is critical for you and your business to make a profit.

Just as important is the timetable. Too many contractors get into trouble because they do not realize or forget how vital this project is to the prospect or they allow there to be confusion as to the timetable. This can easily happen when the prospect is a gabby person and gets sidetracked, or if he is constantly interrupted by his staff or by phone calls while you are in the meeting. Be patient, but <u>do not be afraid to pin your prospect down on deadlines</u>. If he will not or cannot give you definite deadlines, let him know that you cannot go further until you have that information. You cannot afford for your crew and equipment to start the project and then be left hanging while the prospect's company plays around with when they want things done. That is like opening up your wallet and saying to them, "Here, help yourself."

You are trying to help the prospect solve a problem by taking on their project. So, be firm, but at the same time be personable. As a sign of good faith, offer flexibility wherever you can without actually painting yourself into a corner.

Some business owners are so proud of their companies that they go on tangents during the conversation and waste time talking about unrelated topics. Steer your prospect back to sharing the information you need. Keep referring back to your checklist. This will ensure you make the most progress in the shortest amount of time. You will come away with all the details you need to make an informed decision about the prospect, and your potential client will respect you for being knowledgeable and for not taking up too much of his time. If you take him on as a client, you will have already established a good working relationship that will carry through the entire project and beyond.

The secret to successfully "Qualifying Prospects" is consistency. Stick to your checklist. As time goes on, you will probably fine-tune the wording and content of the questions as you discover which questions give you the answers you need. Update your checklist periodically. Tailor it to keep it relevant to both your company's needs and the needs of your current potential clients. This updated checklist will be your best friend as you seek out new clients. Make a habit of using it whenever you communicate with prospects.

Tricks for Taking Good Notes:

Before you meet with your prospect, sit down in a quiet place and brainstorm about what specific information you need in order to judge whether or not you want to take on a potential project. Create a list of keywords to use when meeting with a prospect. In a way, this is similar to the keywords you type in the computer when searching for information online. Specific nouns and verbs will let Google or Yahoo locate the product or other information we are searching for.

Make a list of the keywords that are critical for this particular job. Most general contracting jobs need details, for example, about the site: elevations; locations of electric, water, and sewer lines; soil consistency; road access; etc. You need to know the planned layout, building size, and foundation type. You need to see the blueprints and find out the quality of materials to be used on the job. You get the idea.

Once you have your keywords, formulate them into questions. Remember that "Good questions get good answers." By thinking and planning ahead, you will save yourself the frustration of missing something vital.

As you go through the checklist with your prospect, jot down his answers to your questions. Also, highlight the points that you feel are critical. (Use a highlighter, or underline and place asterisks, etc.) After you are done with your checklist, go back and recap the highlighted points to your prospect. This accomplishes several purposes: it lets your prospect know that you really listened; it allows you to remind him of key points you want to make; and it clears up any misunderstandings, because if you jotted down something incorrectly, your prospect will immediately correct you.

Building Emotion as you Qualify Prospects:

Although meeting a prospect is an exchange of information, it should not be dry and boring. After all, your prospect is excited about his business and you are excited about yours. Your enthusiasm should come through your words, your body language, and your tone of voice. If you are ever going to convince this prospect to <u>want</u> to be your client, you need to create some emotional momentum going from the moment you introduce yourself and shake hands until you shake hands again to close the deal.

From the first moments of your conversation with your prospect, start gauging the emotional connection between the two of you. Right off the bat, you should be asking questions that allow the prospect to explain the problem that he needs solved. Judge whether this prospect is seriously excited about having you help solve that problem or whether he is just "window shopping." Window shoppers, or what I call "bargain hunters," are not yet serious about getting their problems solved. They just want to feel you out to see what you can offer them and at what cost. As you go through your checklist, you will be able to determine early on whether this prospect wants the problem fixed or is window shopping, because if he is not serious, at some point the conversation will stall. Your prospect will not be giving you the information you need to qualify him. Instead you will realize that you are wasting your time. *Do not tell him that!* Just politely tell him that from your perspective it seems that he has still not decided about the details of the project. Let him know to call you when he is ready. Leave your card with the prospect. He may surprise you and start providing you workable details. If this happens, complete your qualification process.

Most times, however, your prospect is excited about bringing you in to do the project. He knows he needs help and is willing to pay for the right contractor to do the job. The two of you will connect, and the enthusiasm the prospect has will propel the meeting forward. You will be getting the answers you are looking for, and he will be thrilled with the products and services you can offer him.

Categorizing your Prospects:

If you are seriously prospecting, before long you will have hundreds of prospects. These are companies that you have contacted in person or cold-called by phone, or companies that gave you their business cards. You may also have compiled a list of potential customers from the Internet, through online local and trade directories, and websites.

If you do not organize these prospects in some way, the sheer numbers will overwhelm you, and you may miss out on the best possibilities while wasting time on longshots.

I prioritize my prospects using a letter code, such as A, B, C, D. Another method would be to assign a two-letter code that lets you know at a glance the prospect's priority. For example:

HP - High Priority

RB - Ready to Buy

DQ - Wants Work Done Quickly

ND - No Deadline Yet / or PU - Project Unscheduled

RF – Referral

DM – Must Talk to Decision-maker

Create any categories and codes that will help you prioritize your prospects. Categorizing your prospects and creating a spreadsheet like Excel will allow you to not only prioritize them, but also to keep track of your progress with each one. Create codes for follow-ups as well. For example, SM – Set Up Meeting, FC – Follow-up Call, CP – Contract Pending, and CS – Contract Signed.

Summary:

<u>Always remember to Qualify before Selling</u>. You may end up qualifying and selling in the same meeting, especially if the prospect is enthusiastic and you can easily determine that his project fits your company like a glove. Most times, however, it is wiser to qualify a prospect using your checklist. Go back to your office, read over your notes, and rate the prospect before going back to make your presentation. You may decide that another prospect is more time-sensitive or is a higher priority and, therefore, should be given the sales presentation first.

If you rush ahead without qualifying the prospect, you may end up doing nothing more than practicing your presentation, because he was not really interested in the first place.

<u>One Last Note</u>:

Do not overcomplicate the qualifying process. Qualifying can be as quick as a two-minute phone call. If you immediately get to talk to the decision-maker, you may get all your qualification questions answered without breaking a sweat. Other times, you will have to be more patient, persistent and willing to have multiple conversations or meetings in order to qualify the prospect. Just make sure you cover all the points on your checklist, take good notes and highlight them, and rate your prospects by category. Then you will be able to judge whether this prospect is a prime candidate for your sales presentation.

<u>My "Blue Light Special" Customer</u>

I am a Christian and have been following the Lord for close to 18 years. The reason why I say this is because we are not supposed to pre-judge people. Over the years, I have tried to make a point not to judge people on appearances alone. Although I am getting better at it, I haven't quite shaken the habit completely.

I met with a potential customer in a very bad part of town. The man got out of the car dressed in a tobacco stained white undershirt and torn, faded blue jeans, which had to be a "Blue Light Special" from K-Mart. I don't know about you, but I couldn't help thinking I was probably wasting my time with this one.

Nevertheless, I approached him with my best smile and a friendly handshake and gave him my card. I asked the right probing questions, measured the job, and asked for the sale. To my surprise, his response was, "How much yah need down to start?" I took a double-take. What? Did I hear that right?

I recovered quickly and said, "I will need half down to start." He said, "Okay, follow me."

I jumped back into my truck and followed his truck around the corner to another house. Same thing: I measured the job, he asked, "How much?" "Okay, follow me."

We went across town to a third house, a two-story that needed some serious TLC. Same exact deal: "How much?" "When can you start?" I told him and noted other issues in the house that would need to be addressed and started explaining them in detail. He stopped me. "How much?" "Here is your check to get started on everything."

To date, I have worked on 14 out of the 63 houses this man owns. Come to find out after working for him since 2009, he made millions in a security company he owned for 30 years, and now likes to invest in real estate. He purchases two houses per year. His hobby is fixing them up to rent.

As contractors, we tend to think of our customers as being a certain way, a certain age. We guesstimate their household income and assume their education. Instead, we should just take a step back and not try to put them into a box. Our clients are individuals with their own goals, achievements, priorities, and personalities. Our job is to do our best to build a relationship with them, respect their expertise, and coordinate with them as a professional friend to get the job done right.

ch: 4

Your Presentation

When you make your presentation to a potential customer, remember that this is *not* a lecture where you do all the talking and your prospect does all the listening. Rather, it is a genuine give-and-take. You need to briefly introduce your company and offer an overview of what you do for customers. Unless your potential customer tells you exactly what he needs, your assumptions could be way off base. <u>Your presentation needs to achieve two goals</u>: 1) Getting your prospect interested by concisely showcasing your company and expertise, and 2) *Immediately* asking questions that prompt your prospect to share specifics about the project. You are not prying unnecessarily; you just need to know certain information in order to help. Your goal is to match your contracting services with the prospect's needs. The better the match, the happier your client will be with the results.

It is all about problem-solving. Your prospect has a specific problem that he wants solved—otherwise he would not be listening to your presentation. He expects that your business can meet his needs. It's up to you, during your presentation, to convince him that you are the right person/company for the job.

<u>Have a list of questions ready before the presentation</u>. You want to find out from your prospect what needs to be done, how extensive

is the job, what is the anticipated time frame for completion, and a ballpark budget figure. As you ask and he answers, take notes. Also, ask clarifying questions so that there are no misunderstandings about details. For example, are you as the contractor responsible for ordering all materials, or is the prospect planning on ordering certain brands or products with specific specs? Make sure that he is aware of your company's minimum quality requirements for the products you install.

Here is where you can promote the benefits of dealing with your company. Once you have a general idea of what the prospect is looking for, you can start listing the benefits that will result if your team does the work—i.e. Dedicated workers, high quality workmanship, superior products, personalized service, etc. Bring out your company brochures or show him your website. This way he can see pictures of projects that your company has recently completed. Discuss recently completed jobs and describe the ways that these projects are similar to the projected one, again reminding him of your company's superior service and quality. Emphasize the fact that you use only top-of-the-line products, so once the job is done, it will last. If you have manufacturers' brochures for products you will use on the project, go through them with him as well.

Keep asking questions as you discuss your company and keep writing down your prospect's answers. The more you understand about what he is expecting from you, the better you will be able to achieve those expectations.

To conclude your presentation, do a quick recap of your presentation's key points . Then, "assume the sale." This means shift gears from fact-finding to going after the job. You believe you can do the job better than your competitors, so let the prospect know how much you believe in your company and your people to do the job right. Ask a couple of questions that he can agree with. This will subconsciously reinforce positive feelings about you and your company. For example: "You said earlier that you are thinking about a two month time frame, right?" (Let him nod or say yes). "Well, given what you have told me, we can easily meet that deadline for you." Then, ask if you can set up a follow-up meeting at the site to determine first-hand what needs to be done. If the prospect reacts positively to this suggestion, you are on your way to landing the job.

If you feel the job is a good match for your company, you can say something like, "Well, my crew and I can be ready to start this project as early as [Tuesday]. Are there any questions you still have that would delay that start date?" This lets you remove objections early on, leaving the prospect without any reasonable excuse to say no to you.

Before you leave, give the prospect your business card and urge him to call or email you with any other questions. Point out your email address and the URL of your website for his convenience, and get his business card and email address if you do not already have them.

Post-Presentation Note: At your office, set up a presentation file that contains not only copies of presentations made previously, but also make a separate list of all the questions you have asked each prospect. You will notice there are certain typical questions that get you key facts you need for most jobs. These questions should form your core repertoire of questions for every job presentation you make. The other questions are mostly job-specific and may fit some prospect projects but not others. Review your list of questions as you prepare each new presentation. This will save you the frustration of trying to remember what worked last time.

Short, Sweet, and To the Point:

Always assume your potential customer is a very busy person and you are lucky the prospect has taken the time out to talk with you. Do not waste his time or irritate him. Your goal is to make him *ecstatic* about hiring you for this contracting job. Keeping your presentation short, sweet, and to the point is how you will accomplish this.

New studies on adult attention spans indicate that the attention span of your potential customer is only 10 minutes. That means you have to cram all your critical information into the first 10 minutes of your meeting with him. Obviously, if you want to emphasize certain key points and clarify details, 10 minutes does not give you much wiggle room.

The solution is what I call "<u>Staggering</u>." An odd term, but effective. Staggering is when you break up your presentation so after you present some information to your prospect, you immediately ask related questions so the prospect senses that you are interested in his expertise and opinions on the matter. Not only will you get the critical answers you need, but you will also extend the prospect's attention span so that he will be actively processing everything you are saying. After the Q&A, pick up with your next point and follow up with another Q&A session, and so on throughout your presentation.

Staggering also builds trust. The more interaction you can get going between yourself and your prospect—the more Q's & A's—the more likely he will trust you, because he appears to be getting to know you. Once you have established this connection, you will become a trusted advisor for all questions relating to the project.

<u>Do not throw around technical terms</u> just to impress your potential customer. It does not work. The prospect will either become overwhelmed or confused by too many technical terms, or he will simply tune you out and you will be talking to a wall. If your technical area of expertise is foreign to most business owners, you have to find a way to enable your prospective customer to relate to and understand what you are saying. Limit technical terms to only those absolutely necessary for the customer's project. Prepare easy-to-understand definitions, and explain the rest in layman's terms—or, in other words, plain English.

This way you will relate to your prospect on his terms and get him to trust you, because what you are saying actually makes sense. A second way to relate to your customer is to give him something to hold. This could be a sample part that you would use in his project. The physical experience of handling the part, turning it over, and looking at it will build trust and help convince the prospect that what you are telling him is valid and as dependable as this part. Occasionally, your perspective and the prospect's perspective will be worlds apart. He may have no interest in the technology that goes into the project. He just wants the project done and done right. In that case, look for other ways to relate to him. For example, maybe he has a family photo on the desk. Compliment him on his beautiful family and mention that your son is trying out for football. Maybe he has a certificate on the wall or a pro team mug on the desk, strike up a conversation to make it apparent you both have a few things in common. Once a prospect senses that you are similar in some way, he will be more willing to really listen to what you have to say.

Types of Presentations

Presentations come in many shapes and sizes. They appeal to different people and different personalities. Be prepared and willing to use whichever type of presentation fits the business owner, the situation, and your purposes at the time.

As you know, the most common type of presentation is the "in-person" presentation. This can be oral, printed, or a PowerPoint. Oral presentations are most effective when they have been mostly or completely memorized, and the contractor does not get flustered if the prospect interrupts with a question. A PowerPoint slide show is a great example of the saying, "One picture is worth a thousand words," because the diagrams, cartoons, and graphs are almost self-explanatory and memorable. The contractor will not miss mentioning anything important, because everything is on the slide show.

Usually a printed presentation booklet forms the basis for an oral or PowerPoint presentation and contains additional details that there is not time to cover during a meeting. Some printed presentations include "screen shots" from the PowerPoint presentation as well.

If the prospect is short on time or wants some preliminary information, email is the way to go. You can give him a quick rundown of your key points in the email and he can respond with questions. Then, email him the answers. This back-and-forth establishes a good preliminary relationship and can be the basis for future meetings. In your email, be sure to include your company's website URL. Make it an active link (blue underlined), so the prospect can click on it and be taken directly to your website. Put your website URL on your business cards, and all brochures and postcards that you send or leave with prospects. Your website alone is a powerful presentation. You do not even have to be present for some prospects to give you the job. You do, however, need to be available by phone and email to answer questions and urge him to consider hiring you and your company.

Never underestimate the effectiveness of a phone call. This is the next best thing to giving a presentation in-person. It has a personal touch and is an efficient way to pass along information to your prospective customer. Always have a phone presentation prepared. This presentation should be a mini version of your in-person presentation. The last thing you want to do is stumble over your words trying to give a presentation to a prospect. Instead, have a copy of your phone presentation by your desk phone and in your pocket, address book or briefcase so it is with you wherever you are when you make or receive the call.

Practicing

Nothing is more embarrassing than being in front of a prospective customer and forgetting your key points. Not many business owners can make an effective presentation without preparation. Most of us, who are experts at our job, still need to practice a presentation so that it flows, hits all the critical points, and does not waste the prospect's time.

Therefore, once you have written your presentation, <u>rehearse it</u>. Rehearse it at work, at home, while driving, in front of a mirror, even into a tape recorder. The more you rehearse your presentation, the more relaxed and convincing you will be.

Successfully making a presentation means <u>memorizing the key points</u>—especially the first phrase of each new point. This way if a prospect asks a question, you will know the first phrase of each point and you will not be thrown off your game.

As you practice your presentation, pretend you are actually talking to a potential customer. Be polite. Practice introducing yourself. Maintain professional-friendly eye contact, and remember to thank the client at the end of your presentation for taking time to meet with you. If the prospect hires you to do the job, let him know that you look forward to working together.

<u>Presentation Tips that Work:</u>

<u>Idea #1:</u>

<u>Holding Practical and Informative Seminars</u>

I recently attended a waterproofing seminar put on by a local paint company. Sixteen contractors and nineteen management companies attended. The food was great, and the presentation was right on the mark, demonstrating what the weather and salty air do to commercial buildings and great ways to maintain properties without spending a fortune.

The paint company also provided an awesome catered lunch, and everyone felt it was a tremendous success.

Afterwards, I asked the company about its success rate and how it prepared for the presentation. The company's principal informed me that the company does a similar presentation every other month all around the county targeting management companies and general contractors that the company currently works for in those areas. He further informed me that the topics covered are all vital to contracting work. Usually about 15-40 people show up. The average total cost for the seminar ranges from $320-$740. This includes $85.00 room rental, $9 per person for food, and $100 for giveaway promotions. The seminar usually results in three to five jobs for the company, depending on the turnout. The average job size is $5,600.00. Not a bad investment, wouldn't you agree?

Since then, I have been setting up similar seminars for local companies and contractors. **Call me direct for details if you would like to participate or want to conduct a seminar in your area. Justin (727) 644-0160.**

Idea #2:

Community Event called "Touch a Truck" for Kids

One day I noticed that an electrical company was in town showing off their clean "state-of-the-art" truck and letting kids climb around and explore items on the truck (with supervision, of course). The guys were giving away magnets and other promotional items, too. More importantly, I personally saw the owner give out over 80 business cards in a short period of time. Why didn't I think of that? I could get free advertising, build rapport with the community, and get my contact information into the hands of dozens of potential customers. All I had to do was clean up my truck, stock up on a few trinkets and balloons, park it in a popular spot, and mingle. You can bet that I duplicated that promotional method more than once! Presenting yourself to thousands of friendly people is a priceless way to build your business.

Idea #3:

<u>Using Social Media to help Market your Brand</u>

Social media, whether you use Facebook or LinkedIn, is a powerful magnet to draw customers to your company. Of course, before you start promoting your business on social media, <u>make sure that your profile is up-to-date</u> and that you have posted photos, a concise description of what you do, and even some coupons that customers can use for contracting projects.

Once your Facebook or LinkedIn page is set up the way you want it, <u>take advantage of the advanced search features</u> found on social media websites so you can search for companies or individuals in your marketplace and start connecting. This is how you build your contact lists using the Internet. It's easy; just follow these steps:

1. CLICK the Advanced Search feature;

2. INSERT a Keyword (your prospects' fields/businesses) in the search box;

3. SEARCH the Zip Code or City you want to target;

4. CONNECT with the contacts that fit your criteria, using the tools in this book;

5. SEND Valuable Information to your list every month to build their trust and interest.

These are just some of the ideas that are covered in more detail on my website www.ContractorsNetworking.com

ch: 5

Negotiation Script

Once you have completed your initial presentation and your prospect is seriously considering your product or service, you need to move seamlessly into the <u>Negotiation Phase</u>.

The Negotiation Phase is where you re-state your key points in a way that makes your prospect agree that each point is a right fit for the project and business objectives. In order to do this, you need to make sure you keep your client's needs central to the discussion. Plowing through and repeating your key reasons why this prospect should hire you for the job will backfire. Your prospect already heard your presentation. He does not need a repeat performance. What he really wants to know is how your particular service or products will dovetail with the project's needs. This means you must be keenly aware of those needs and how you can fulfill them.

The only way you can be aware of your prospect's needs is to do some preliminary preparation. Your preparation will determine whether or not you can convert this prospect into a happy and loyal client. Long before you meet with him to give your presentation, research the company and learn as much as possible about the kind of work the company does, how the prospect approaches projects, and what expectations he has for vendors and other contractors. Some of this vital information can be gleaned from the company's Facebook and LinkedIn pages, as well as talking with other professionals who know this business owner.

As you research and gather information, start matching up this company's priorities with the services your company offers. Turn these into bullet points in your notes so that you can quickly reference and integrate them into your negotiations. With this written agenda handy, you can avoid forgetting a key point that might make or break the deal.

You will not be able to get all your negotiation information from social media and or talking with other professionals. The rest and often the most critical information will become apparent as you make your presentation. Make sure you <u>continue asking questions as you give your presentation.</u> As we discussed earlier, your presentation should be a give-and-take experience, where you ask open-ended questions and encourage the business owner to talk about the business, the approach, the expectations, the business' goals and objectives for this particular project. Take down notes as he talks. Insert this critical information into your bullet-point agenda. Now as you proceed with the Negotiation Phase, you can weave in this information and match your services with the prospect's exact needs. Once the prospect realizes that you are a perfect fit, he will agree to hire you for the job.

Suppose that you get to the end of your presentation but feel uncertain as to how your company can meet this prospect's unique needs, whether it is tight scheduling, specific material brands or having enough manpower. Never try to "wing it" with negotiations; instead, try to make the sale on the spot. There is no shame in leveling with the prospect and saying that although you would like to get started right away, you have several concerns that need to be addressed before starting the job. Start asking the questions. If you still are not getting workable answers, close the meeting by thanking him for his time and let him know that you want to run this by the experts on your crew to see how well you can accommodate his plans. Instead, you could let him know that you need some time to come up with a couple of proposal options that would meet his needs better than a general one-size-fits-all proposal.

As you meet with a prospect, you may discover that you are really out of your depth as far as knowledge of the technical details critical to the project. Don't panic. Everything today is so specialized; there is no such thing as a "Jack of all trades" anymore. Do not feel inadequate or inferior because you do not understand what he is talking about. You are an expert in your field. This may or may not overlap with your prospect's specific field. If your prospect starts rattling off technical terms specific to his company, you have a couple of face-saving options:

1. Stop him politely and admit that you are not familiar with the technical terms being used. Remind the prospect that your expertise is in a different area. Ask if he doesn't mind talking in "layman's terms" so you understand exactly what is being said, because you do not want to misunderstand him. Most business owners will accommodate you and appreciate your honesty and feel complimented that you are acknowledging their own expertise in the field.

2. Ask the prospect if he has some specs or other materials that you can take with you to look over with your crew. Let him know you will be back in touch shortly with a proposal specifically designed to fit the project.

Continuing your Negotiations:

Always be honest with both yourself and your prospect as to what you can do and how well you can meet his expectations. Encourage him to let you know if there is some flexibility in the timetable or product specs. Let the prospect know where you can accommodate him and which terms (for example, payment terms) are set in stone. Negotiations are all about trying to give the other person as much "wiggle room" as possible so both parties are satisfied with the arrangement. This kind of negotiating also builds trust that can last far beyond the length of the project.

As you negotiate, you do not want to simply repeat the features and benefits of your products and services. You do, however, need to show how they meet the prospect's very specific needs. Take each product and service offered one-by-one. If you can demonstrate each product and service visually, all the better. While you do this, emphasize the differences between your company and your competition. Be aware of what your competitors offer and how you outshine them in quality, durability, workmanship, warranties, customer service, etc. Knowing this information will create value for the prospect. He starts to see how you are the only contractor who can do the job right. As he agrees with you on each point, the prospect starts to own the process. This prepares the prospect to respond positively to your closing.

Overcoming Objections before Closing:

One critical step you must take before you begin your closing is to Clear Away Objections. Even if you have "wowed" your prospect with your presentation and negotiation, you will never be sure that there are not some lingering doubts in the back of the prospect's mind unless you ask. So Ask!

One of the best ways to get your prospect to reveal any objections is to say, "What is keeping you from signing this contract right now?" This will force most business owners to admit their objections out loud. Maybe they are worried about affording the cost, are not ready to make a commitment, need more information, or have to run it by their financial partners. Even after you think you have heard every objection and excuse, someone will give you one you have not heard before. Your greatest asset is your ability to listen. Listen to their objections and do not be quick to react. Absorb what they are saying and decide if they are legitimate objections. Maybe you can clarify a point that will eliminate the objection and leave the prospect realizing that you are offering the best service and the best deal.

When a prospect objects by claiming that a relative (father or brother, for example) has been in the business for years and said this or that, just nod your head and act impressed. Then, take the conversation back to specific features and benefits that meet the project's needs and ask if he is comfortable with getting that kind of service.

One common way prospects put off committing is to question your product or service, claiming they read somewhere that the material you planned to use has a flaw or that some other contractor said in his ad that he would do the job for $300 less. Counter these objections by saying that we cannot believe everything we see in print, especially ads. It is better to rely on facts. Point out some specific facts you mentioned earlier, or, if you have copies of reviews or testimonials from happy clients, these could tip things in your favor.

A second way prospects put off committing is the closed-minded objection of not being interested. Do not let this throw you. Instead, come back with a concerned look and ask what would make them interested. Ask what it is that bothers them about the service you are offering. Maybe they really do not have time to deal with it right now, or they are worried about the economy and the affordability. Their answers may give you an opening to close the deal. Even if you cannot get a prospect to budge from his position, at least you will find out what the phrase "not interested" could signify so you will be better prepared to counter it next time.

It is likely at some point during your presentation, your prospect will quibble about the price of your product or service. If you have been told point blank, "I think your price is too high," it is usually an indication that you did not convey sufficient value to the prospect. Most people are willing to spend more money if they believe they are getting more quality features or long-term benefits from the item. If it is unclear that they will be getting more, they will avoid committing to the sale.

If the prospective homeowner or business is excited about what you are offering, they will usually weigh the factors and determine that the additional cost is worth it. But, suppose the prospect is not in love with the product, but recognizes that he needs it. In this case, he will be hemming and hawing about whether he should wait and look around for a better price or whether he should save the time and trouble and just go with you, since you are right there in the office. In either case, he is a disgruntled prospect, and this type of potential customer is reluctant and who will be the first to criticize your workmanship or another aspect of the job.

You want to avoid reluctant customers. Instead, ramp up your effort to help the prospect understand the <u>value</u> that he is getting by hiring you for the job. <u>Whether your prospect's bottom line is a factor depends on the perception of how valuable your services are</u>. He will happily pay more if he believes the product or service provides something he values.

For example, if your prospect objects saying, "Your price is too high," immediately empathize with him and say something like, "I totally agree with you, Mr. _____, this investment may be higher than you expected." Or "I understand how you feel, my last customer felt the same way." Then proceed, "The question is, is this your only objection to what I am proposing?" If the prospect says yes, you can go on to reiterate the value that this product will have for him. Often during a presentation, the prospect gets a little overwhelmed and misses key points you make, or forgets some of them. Your point may not have come across clearly. It never hurts to repeat features and benefits. Just make sure you are directly linking each feature or benefit to one of the prospect's needs. Help him make the connections. Then he will decide for himself that your product or service is what is specifically needed and worth the extra cost.

If the prospect still insists that the price is too high, ask what else he believes should be included for the price. If he says a competitors quote is lower, ask what the competitor is offering that you haven't mentioned. When you get down to specifics, often the prospect will back down, because he really is just trying to haggle you down on the price. If he has a genuine concern, see how you can accommodate him, or point out something you already said that satisfies the issue.

This is the perfect opportunity to discuss specific features or find out what the prospect likes about your competitor other than the price. Now, highlight what makes you different, better, more dependable, and trustworthy. Mention a testimonial from a happy client who had a project similar to your prospect's job.

This will start to eliminate any doubts your prospect harbors, one-by-one. These lingering doubts are the basis for the prospect's objections. Cut the objections off at the root, until there is no logical reason for your prospect to decline the sale.

If you have done all you can to portray the value of your company as opposed to your competitor, and you have cleared away all reasonable objections, briefly cover your main points again and transition to your closing strategy.

<u>Closing</u>:

Remember, when you are trying to close your negotiation, the purpose is more than just getting a signed contract. A successful contract means both parties benefit and are satisfied with the agreement. Your ultimate goal is a "Win-Win." If your prospect is not happy with the terms of the agreement or is uncomfortable with part of the contract, you can be sure that he will be very critical of every aspect of the job and you may end up with a bad experience.

When starting your final phase, the closing, keep the conversation casual. Put the prospect at ease by being at ease yourself. It does not matter how much you have riding on this sale, if you are stressed about forcing the outcome, it will show in your tone of voice and your body language. The prospect will respond less to what you say and more to what he perceives as nervousness or desperateness.

Instead, have an open dialogue with the prospect. Think of it as a casual Ping-Pong game that is both engaging and relaxing. Listen carefully and make continuous eye contact. Casually ask the prospect if he has any questions and answer them in a straightforward manner. Ask how the prospect sees your company helping achieve his goals and what he feels your team will do for him.

Once the prospect expresses this, he will be ready to hire you for the job. Now is the time to express your commitment to the work, the deadlines, and the materials used.

Asking for the Sale

Once you and the prospect are in agreement on all terms, and there are no questions left unanswered, now is the time to be confident and - Ask for the sale. Bring out the contract and go over it with the prospect, making sure he understands and agrees with each part as previously discussed in the "Closing" phase. Then, offer him the pen to sign.

Special Note:

It is true that some prospects are not a good fit, so you will not sign up every prospect, but you might be surprised later: If after that prospect gets additional quotes or has a bad experience with another contractor, he may call you up out of the blue and ask if your offer is still on the table. If you have done a good job of presenting value and eliminating objections, your business will appear as a shining star compared to your competitors and prospects will remember you for future projects.

Negotiating with a Retired Attorney

My all-time favorite <u>negotiation story</u> started with a roundtable of condominium owners who wanted to replace the roofs on their individual units. You can imagine the pressure I felt: 12 different personalities all focusing on my presentation. I seldom get nervous—just occasionally uncomfortable when I don't quite feel the connection. This, however, made me nervous. I wanted to do this right.

For my jobs, I use a three-page contract written by a construction attorney, which I have been using for the past three years. It is simple, clean and easy to understand. I normally finish reviewing the contract in a matter of minutes and I am sure to ask if the prospect's have any questions. Most times there are no questions. I figured that this negotiation would be no different. Not *this* time! The bookkeeper for the condominium group, a retired attorney, pulled out a hefty file folder and dramatically flipped through the pockets of the folder. He stopped at the tab that said "Roofs." I saw a 23-page packet, and I wondered, "What on earth is this?" He started by asking some questions while flipping through the pages. Nearly an hour later, he finished with his contract negotiations. He had contract sections that thoroughly covered every detail—even things I had never even considered. It was a perfect fit for the project and met my criteria as well. I was impressed.

I guiltily slid my one-size-fits-all contract back into my briefcase and signaled to him that I was ready to sign. We both signed his contract and started the project. <u>Negotiation</u> means covering the little stuff as well as the big stuff. Typically both parties haggle back and forth on certain issues, but this time, it was a well-put-together contract. That was the last time I will ever assume I know everything that needs to be in a contract!

ch: 6

Recognizing When to Close?

It is easy to be too involved in your sales presentation—discussing products, installation, warranties, and investment—that you get distracted and forget to ask for the sale. Especially, if your potential client is very talkative. The discussion could get so far off target that there is no way to swing it back gracefully to your close without seeming contrived. You do NOT want to be in this situation.

Let's rewind a bit and see whether we could have prevented the above sales blunder. Everything has flowed beautifully so far. The prospect has been with you each step of the way, agreeing with you regarding what is needed for the project and what you can do for him. The schedule seems workable. So far, you have answered all of his questions, and the testimonials of your happy clients have made an impact. You sense that you and the prospect are on the same page.

How do you lead into your closing? At what point do you determine it is time to ask for the sale? *How* do you determine that it is time? Here are **Six Examples** of customer questions and responses that show you it is time to close the presentation and ask for the sale. Make sure you have first completed all other steps outlined in Chapters 1 - 5 of this Handbook:

1. If your prospect <u>compliments the product or service you are offering</u>, take that as a green light to start your closing. He might say, "I really like this…." or "You know, this _____ seems very well made." Immediately, reinforce his opinion by highlighting a feature related to the product and at the same time complimenting the prospect's expertise on the matter. For example, if he says, "I really like the type of construction that you use in your window sills." You answer back, "Well, the double reinforcement complements the sturdiness you are planning in those walls. Your building will be in a high-wind area with few trees. From what I can see on your plans, you are making a good choice." From here, you can ask for the sale, because your prospect has already committed to the superiority of your product and acknowledges it is a good fit with his plans, and you have confirmed that fact.

2. If <u>your prospect asks a technical question</u> like, "How thick is the underlayment?" or "What grade steel do you typically use?" Specific technical questions are a good indicator that your potential client has leaped ahead and is already considering you as his contractor. As you have been talking, he has mentally immersed himself in the project and is anticipating the details of the job. You do not need to convince him with more sales talk at this stage. Just ask for the sale.

3. If the prospect approaches you and <u>wants to review your proposal</u>, most likely, he has seriously considered it and has specific detail questions. He might say, "Tell me again how the pipes are going to be installed," or "What type of warranty do I get?" Answer these questions and ask if there is anything else

that needs confirming regarding the proposal. If the prospect seems satisfied with your answers, ask for the sale.

4. Another green light is when <u>the prospect nods and agrees that all of his concerns have been addressed</u> satisfactorily, "I think you have covered everything" or "No, I don't have any more questions." At this point, you can confidently ask for the sale.

5. <u>When your potential customer starts asking about</u> investment or payment, take out the paperwork and pen. When he asks, "How much do you need to start" or "Can I use a credit card?" he is fully committed, and you just need to clarify the initial deposit, the payment schedule, and have him sign the contract.

6. Always listen and interact with your prospect. Do not be so tied to your presentation that you fail to <u>realize when your potential customer is trying to move your presentation along, because he is ready to sign</u>. He might say something like, "I understand that part. Let's talk about _____." Adjust your presentation to address how ready the prospect is to commit. Of course, when you hear the words "Okay, give me the pen, where do I sign?" - you are home free!

For your convenience, here are the above clues at a glance:

Quick Guide of Clues indicating it's Time to Close:

1. The potential customer is complimenting what you are offering.

    i.   "I really like this….."

    ii. "This ___ looks very well made."

2. The potential customer is asking technical questions.

    i. "How thick is the underlayment?"

    ii. "What grade steel do you use?"

3. The potential customer wants to review your proposal.

    i. "Tell me again how the pipes are going to be installed."

    ii. "What type of warranty do I get?"

4. The potential customer's concerns have all been met.

    i. "I think you have covered everything."

    ii. "No, I don't have any more questions."

5. The potential customer starts asking about investment or payment.

    i. "How much do you need to start?"

    ii. "Can I use a credit card?"

6. The potential customer starts moving your presentation along.

    i. "I understand that part. Let's talk about___."

    ii. "Okay, give me the pen. Where do I sign?"

Listen and watch for these clues. Do not miss an opportunity to make a sale.

Closing the Sale: The Salesman's Drug of Choice.

My mentor taught me how to close a sale and overcome objections, which I have laid out systematically for you in this handbook. I have also given you clues indicating when to close. I can remember how I felt, coming back to the office fresh from sales meetings and presentations pitching services. Some days, I would come in with my head held high as I dropped several contracts on the desk, feeling like the "top dog." Other times, weeks might go by with nothing to show for my efforts but disappointing prospecting and meetings with no signatures.

My first year as a contractor, I earned approximately $9,126.00. Yep, that comes to a whopping $3.50 an hour. My bank account was hurting, but what I learned that year was invaluable. I would share stories with my mentor about meeting with a company to discuss a certain project and, without fail, my mentor would ask if I was "hungry." Of course, I was hungry—I was always hungry. At the time, I thought he was talking about food because he would invite the entire office out to eat on my dollar. My tab would be around $80.00. Then, my mentor would press me to tell my stories to the group. He would crack up laughing at my stories. I never understood why, and he would always say, "You'll see someday." Well, "someday" finally came, and I understood. Thank you, Jerry Freeman, for taking the time to invest in me and for believing I have what it takes. I owe my start and a good measure of my success to you.

ch: 7

Referrals

Referrals:

Did you know referral business has a 60% higher closing rate than non-referral business? There are good reasons for this:

When a prospect is referred to your company, <u>your credibility is increased</u>. People tend to believe what others say, so when they hear that previous clients had a good experience with your company and they recommend you, you already have a better chance of landing the job than a company that is randomly picked out of the phone book. This is another reason why it is so critical to have reviews and testimonials posted on your website, Facebook, and LinkedIn pages. Referral services such as Angie's List and HomeAdvisor.com are booming these days for this very reason. People hesitate to hire just anyone to do a project, but are more likely to depend on the recommendation of someone who has dealt with your company before and has had a positive experience.

Depending exclusively on <u>passive referrals</u> from Angie's List is not enough to bring in the number of new clients you need for your business to flourish. <u>You need to be proactive</u>. You need to think outside the box!

"Thinking outside the box" means taking advantage of the credibility you have already established through past successful jobs and letting that credibility attract new business for your company. Customers who have had a great experience working with you already trust you. That trust can be contagious, and their referrals can prompt other businesses to hire you for the job.

Here are some effective ways to get referrals:

- If you are meeting with your customer after the job or following up with them by phone, do not hesitate to ask, "Would you recommend us to others?" Tell them you want to know how the experience was from their end. Ask, "What did we do right and what can we improve upon?" Jot down the answers. Ask if you may use them as a reference and don't forget to thank them for their honesty.

- If you are in a casual setting with colleagues, association members, or friends, ask specific questions to get them considering why they would recommend your company. For example, "Would you say that we are a dependable company?" and "From your experience with us, would you recommend us to a friend who needs contracting work done?"

- One way to ask for a referral is to simply ask for the best way to keep in contact with them. Then, tell the customer that you would like to use them as a referral and need a point of contact person for other companies to call for the reference.

- Mail a card to your existing customer as both a "Thank you" note and a brief survey that he can quickly fill out and return to you. One of the questions on the survey should be, "Would you recommend this company to a friend or colleague who needs similar contracting work done?" Even add a place for them to write in a referral. Make sure that the survey is self-addressed and stamped, so the client can simply drop it in the mailbox.

After a client sends you a referral or after your completed survey card has been returned to you, always follow up with a "thank you" by email, mail, phone, or in person when you happen to be in the area. Your thank you will confirm how professional your company is and it will make the client feel confident in having referred you to a friend.

Believe it or not, <u>the people who refer you to friends and local businesses are your best "Sales Force."</u> These people are marketing for you while you are busy on the job. They are promoting your contracting work whenever they meet other people. Moreover, they are marketing your company *for free*—out of the goodness of their heart. So, <u>what are you doing to maintain your referral business</u>? Your referral "sales force" will continue working for you *if* you stay in contact and show your appreciation. Make it a point to keep building rapport with your former customers over the years. Put them on your newsletter, mailing, or emailing list and keep them abreast of your company's upcoming events. Keep sending them useful information on Facebook, in your newsletter, and in email attachments. Stop by and visit once in a while to see how they are doing. The success of your contracting company depends on referrals. Make the task of <u>growing a referral "sales force"</u> as much a priority for your business as completing projects on time. This will constantly fill your pipeline with potential customers and give your company the best chance for success.

<u>Coaching your Happy Customer on a Good Referral:</u>

Once you have done a great contracting job and made a customer happy, it is critical you get a referral from him that can bring in more customers.

Most contractors assume that *any* referral from a satisfied customer is a good referral. Consider which sounds better—Example #1 or Example #2 below:

Example #1: "Bob did a great job on repairing my faucet. Give Bob a call at #."

Example #2: "My faucet was leaking all over my cabinets, making a real mess. I called Bob to help with the faucet and he was out within minutes. He stopped the leaking water from ruining my house and repaired the faucet in no time. I trust Bob to handle my plumbing. Here is his #."

You definitely want your customer telling the second story. This is by far the more effective referral. Why? Because it has many more details, it is personalized, and it helps potential customers identify with the happy customer. The specific details in Example #2 above are irrefutable facts that create trust when hearing or reading the story. The happy customer's personal touch in telling what happened makes the story real. This type of referral also allows prospects to identify with the calamity and mess of a leaking faucet and the feeling of relief when it is fixed by an expert who does the job right.

Facts tell and stories sell. Helping your customer relay a compelling message about your work results in an effective referral.

The question is: How do you get your customer to share the more descriptive—and effective—story?

First, you need to help the customer establish the story by reminding your customer of how you interacted with him to resolve the situation. He had a problem, you provided a solution, and he is happy with the result:

1. PROBLEM: My faucet was leaking all over my cabinets.

2. SOLUTION: Bob was at my house within minutes and stopped the water.

3. RESULT: Bob fixed my faucet. I trust Bob with my plumbing.

Now, how should this customer refer you to others? There are six steps that make a referral effective:

Step 1: Your happy customer refers your company to someone he knows.

Step 2: Your happy customer lets you know that he just referred you to someone.

Step 3: You thank your customer for referring you and ask him when is the best time to contact the referral or if that person plans to contact you.

Step 4: You research the referral. That way, when you contact the referral or the referral contacts you, you have an idea of who the prospect is and what his needs might be.

Step 5: When the referral contacts you or when you contact the referral, schedule an appointment. (Immediately, start your Qualifying process with the referral, asking questions, taking notes, etc.)

Step 6: Provide professional feedback to your customer. Get back with the customer who referred you the work, and let him know how your meeting went. Thank him again for the referral.

Helping Customers Refer Business to You:

Referrals will not happen if they are complicated or cumbersome. Give your happy customers easy options for giving a referral. In today's fast-paced life, some of your referrals will be person–to-person. Others can be accomplished by phone, text message, mail, or even via the Internet.

Person-to-person referrals often have the greatest response, because the project is fresh in the customer's mind, and he will personally relay excitement over having found a contractor who did the job so well. To encourage person-to-person referrals, verbally share some guidelines with your satisfied customer so that he shares the story effectively. Use the PROBLEM, SOLUTION, RESULT format discussed above.

To make referring easier for your customers, have a small card or half sheet prepared so you can hand it out before you finish the job. I call this my cheat sheet. It gives the customer a summary on your ideal customers, what your company is looking for, and how to overcome common objections. If all else fails, have your customers tell their PROBLEMS, the SOLUTIONS you provided, and the RESULTS. Also, there should be room on your cheat sheet for the names, phone numbers and email addresses for a couple of referrals. Make sure your business contact information is listed as well. This type of referral card can be used for any kind of referral. It makes it easy for the customers to jot down their stories before forgetting them and helps the customers share the best version of their story. Ask your customers to get back with you by phone or email if they refer you to anyone.

Suggest that your customers text or email their friends and other people who might need your services. If you have a website or Facebook page, reserve a spot for feedback and referrals, so your customers have a convenient way to share their PROBLEMS, SOLUTIONS and RESULTS, so they can quickly refer their friends, family, and colleagues. Online referrals provide fast responses and are a great way to get more prospecting leads. Remember to provide your customers with your website URL.

Referrals are a two-way street:

A successful contractor should not only get referrals, but should give them as well. Your willingness to give referrals to other contractors and businesses will enhance your own reputation and credibility. Always research the contractors before you offer to refer them. If a contractor you refer does a bad job, you will lose credibility. If a contractor you refer does a great job, your credibility will increase. The only way you can know which fellow contractors are trustworthy and dependable is to get to know them and their work. Networking is an ideal way to accomplish this. Participating in social media is another. Customers' opinions fly fast and loose on Facebook and Twitter, and you will be able to separate the poor contractors from the outstanding ones pretty quickly. Angie's List and reviewing the contractors' own websites will also give you clues regarding the contractors' capabilities.

Referrals act as a community's business conscience. What customers really think is reflected in the positive and negative referrals that a contractor receives. If your company has integrity, high ethics, and does the job well, those referrals will help to catapult your business to success.

Special Notes:

1.   Some contractors try to depend on only "word-of-mouth" to market their businesses. This method has worked for centuries to prove the credibility and reliability of a company. It is still an effective marketing method, but word-of-mouth from one happy client to his neighbor will not cut it in today's competitive world. There are not enough neighbors hanging over their fences touting your company.

2.   Social media is the new way to make "word-of-mouth" work for you. With Twitter, Facebook, Pinterest, LinkedIn and YouTube, your customers can broadcast the great job you did by posting their reviews on your website and commenting on your articles. You can even create a website video or YouTube video with interviews from your customers. By making it easy for your customers to share their opinions, you will get "word-of-mouth" benefits!

3.   Finally, treat your referred prospect like every potential customer. Remember to go through all the steps for Qualifying the prospect, gathering information, etc. You may have gained some of the answers through your back-and-forth emails or Facebook/LinkedIn communications, but you still need to verify that information and

make sure the prospect's statements are specific to this project and not just general.

The Next-Generation Salesman

I recently picked up my five-year-old son from kindergarten. He asks me every day if we have to go anywhere before we head to the house. Usually, he is hoping we can run by the local bakery or McDonald's. Today was the usual, "Daddy, where are we going? Do you have anything to do before we go home?" I explained to my son that I had to make a stop and meet a customer before heading home. His question was, "Daddy, what's a customer?" "Well, son," I answered, "customers are Daddy's friends who help make our business great." His response was, "Cool, can I help make our business great?" I explained to him that when we got to the customer's house, I would be meeting with grown-ups and I needed him to mind his manners.

He has been to stops with me before and has seen me interact with customers many times.

This time was a little different. He made up his mind to help. He grabbed my business card, clipboard, and a pen. When we arrived, he hopped out and went up to the customer who met us in the driveway. He announced his name, "Hi, my name is Justin," and handed my business card to the customer. They shook hands, and the customer responded, "Nice to meet you. My name is Anne." He responded, "Hello, Anne, you have a nice home. Please, tell me what the problem is." Meanwhile, I was grabbing my tape measure, digital camera, and brochure out of my truck and hurrying to catch up.

Anne started to explain to him that she has problems with the roof leaking in the back, and she had a bucket under the drips that kept coming down from the ceiling.

His response: "Oh, no. Let's go check it out." They started to make their way to the back of the house with me following. We got to the back room and Justin looked at the bucket and the plaster ceiling. He said, "You know, I have this same problem at my house. My daddy always says he is too busy to fix our leaks." He and the customer both look over at me, "Daddy do you have time to fix this leak?"

I was still in shock watching my five-year old son in action. What was next? Negotiation or Closing? He had just gone through my entire introduction, complimented the house, found the problem (the leak), empathized with the customer, and asked if I could fix the customer's problem. I cleared my throat and answered, "I'm sure we can. I just need to investigate up in the attic and take a look at your roof." Anne showed me the way.

While I examined the attic and roof, I listened to my son's muffled voice through the floorboards. He continued building rapport with the customer and asking all kinds of questions.

After I finished measuring, taking photos, and analyzing the problem, I came back down the ladder and into the living room where Anne was entertaining Justin. I told Anne that I wanted to go over the pictures with her and give her an estimate. Justin asked if he could stay and listen. Anne and I agreed and we went over everything page by page. I noticed some hesitation on her part when it came to the investment, and Anne stated that she wanted another opinion before deciding.

We ended up not getting the sale, but I was so proud of my son. When we got back in the truck, I asked him where he had learned all this? His only answer was, "Can we go to McDonald's now?" His observations of me during interactions told him to smile, be friendly, make eye contact, and ask questions. How many of us stress out unnecessarily over sales calls, making them more complicated than they have to be? If a young child can put a customer at ease and build trust, we should be able to handle it without batting an eye!

ch: 8

Conclusion

A successful contracting business involves more than simply being the best in your field. You need to know how to attract new clients and how to promote your business. The competition out there is fierce, so you need to be well-equipped as a competitor.

This is why I have made videos available to you on my website, www. ContractorsNetworking.com. Here is a quick summary of this handbook's key points, so you can keep the most critical concepts in mind as you prospect:

<u>Reach out to Possible Customers:</u>

In today's fast-paced world, the growth of your business depends on <u>meeting people where they are</u>. Set up <u>in-person</u>, one-on-one meetings and attend local networking events. Call prospects by <u>phone</u>, connect with <u>emails</u>, send <u>text messages</u>, and use <u>Facebook, LinkedIn, and Twitter</u>. Save time by using the same basic script for your phone calls, emails, and social media. Your goal is to <u>make a powerful first impression</u>. This means always being prepared to talk about your business and letting your own genuine enthusiasm show through to your prospect.

Qualifying:

"Qualifying" is the system you should use to weed out potential clients that are a poor fit for you and your company and will end up costing extra time and money. Always remember to Qualify before Selling.

Qualify each of your prospects by running through a pre-planned set of probing questions with them. This is your "checklist." These questions allow you to get a feel for what the proposed project is; what expectations the prospect has for you; and what materials, specs, and timelines he requires.

Your Checklist should contain:

- Contact Information. Find out who is the decision-maker or who are the decision-makers.

- Project Details. Encourage your prospect to talk about the project, so you understand its purpose, its scope, the equipment and manpower needed, and the timeline for various aspects of the project. Ask about flexibility and let the prospect know your flexibility and other deadlines.

- Take Extensive Notes. Before you even meet with your prospect, jot down specific keywords that you want information about in order to judge whether or not you want to take on the project. Turn the keywords into questions, so the conversation hits each topic you feel is vital to the project. During the meeting, jot down his answers to your questions. Underline or highlight the answers that you feel are critical.

- Do not be afraid to show Emotion as you Qualify Prospects. This is how you get your prospect excited about hiring you and establish a trusting relationship with him. Your own enthusiasm and integrity should come through your words, your body language, and your tone of voice.

- <u>Categorize your Prospects by Interest Level</u>. Right after your meeting or phone call, rate your prospect by category. This way, you will be able to judge whether this prospect is a prime candidate for your sales presentation.

<u>The Presentation:</u>

<u>Your Presentation needs to achieve two goals</u>: 1) Grabbing your prospect's attention by concisely showcasing your company and expertise, and 2) *Immediately* asking questions that encourage your prospect to share specifics about the project. Prepare <u>a list of questions about the project before the presentation</u>. As you ask your questions and he answers, jot down the answers. <u>Also, ask clarifying questions,</u> so there are no misunderstandings about project details.

Once you have a general idea of the prospect's needs, <u>promote the benefits he will gain by dealing with *your* company</u>. Have a few brochures handy or show him your website. <u>Do not throw around technical terms</u> just to impress your potential customer. Keep your message simple and clear.

<u>Utilize the technique of "Staggering."</u> "Staggering" is breaking up your presentation so after you give some information to your prospect, you immediately ask related questions. This back-and-forth interaction makes the presentation much more interesting, keeps his attention, and lets him feel you really value his expertise and opinions.

<u>To close your presentation, do a quick recap</u> of the key points of your presentation. Then, "<u>assume the sale</u>." Say something like, "Well, my crew and I can be ready to start this project as early as [Tuesday]. Are there any questions you still have that would delay that start date?"

The prospect's answer will let you know if you should move to the Negotiation Phase, or whether you need to allow more time to think about it. If there is an insurmountable reason why you cannot start immediately, then offer your prospect your business card and urge him to call or email you with any other questions.

There are several types of Presentations for you to choose from. Be flexible in deciding which type or combination to use and when to use them. In-person presentations can be oral, printed, or a PowerPoint. Emails let you start building a relationship with the prospect before ever meeting. In the email, prepare a quick rundown of key points, encourage the prospect to email you back with questions, and respond quickly with the answers. A phone call is always the next best thing to In-person presentations. Phone calls have a personal touch and are efficient ways to pass along information to your prospective customers. Always have your phone presentation prepared beforehand, so you do not skip anything critical.

Whatever format you use for your presentation, Practice, Practice, Practice until it rolls off of your tongue. It will become as natural as talking to your best friend, and that is how it should be.

The Negotiation Phase:

This is where you re-state your key points so your prospect agrees with each one. Re-stating does *not* mean using the exact same wording that you used earlier in your presentation. Instead, re-phrase your key points to demonstrate how your particular services or products dovetail with the prospect's needs. You must, therefore, be keenly aware of those needs and how you can fulfill them.

Always be honest with both yourself and your prospect regarding what you can do and how well you can meet the requirements. Negotiating means determining where you both have some flexibility regarding timetables and product specs.

<u>Six Ways to Know that it is Time to Close</u>:

If your prospect does one of the following after you finish giving your presentation, move immediately into your closing. If he:

1. Compliments the product or service you are offering;

2. Asks a technical question;

3. Wants to review your proposal;

4. Agrees that all his concerns have been addressed;

5. Starts asking about investment or payment; or

6. Seems eager to sign the contract.

<u>The Closing</u>:

<u>Your goal during closing is to get your prospect to commit.</u>

To accomplish this you need to:

- Observe your prospect's body language;

- Clear up any remaining objections;

- Confirm answers to your qualifying questions; and

- Ask for signature and payment.

Remind your prospect that you are competent and knowledgeable about each aspect of the job by briefly reviewing your company's strengths and stating exactly what you are offering. Confirm all project timelines and payment schedules, making sure that he is on board with every detail.

Then, confidently say, "Let me get the paperwork." Pull out the contract and all approval forms, including the signature-summaries page. Be sure you are aware of other supervisors, etc., who also need to sign off on some of the documentation. Schedule appointments to meet with any other supervisors for that purpose.

Overcoming Objections:

As you give your presentation and closing, always anticipate that your prospect will have objections to hiring you. The type of objection will tell you how serious he is about having you do the project. Listen closely to the objection and do not be too quick to react. Decide if it is a legitimate objection that will dissolve if you clarify a few points and remind him of how well your company meets this particular need. If the objection is price, review the benefits and quality you are providing. If he is not ready to make a commitment, ask questions to find out why and put this prospect on the back burner for re-contacting at a later date.

One of the best ways to get your prospect to reveal any objections is to ask, "What is keeping you from signing this contract right now?" This will force most business owners to admit their objections out loud. Once the prospect reveals any hesitations, you can address them.

Referrals:

Think outside the box regarding referrals.

Ask for the referral. Consult the handbook's process and step-by-step guide on how and when to ask for referrals.

Utilize happy customers as a "Sales Force."

How should happy customers refer you business? There are six steps that make a referral effective:

<u>Step 1</u>: Your happy customer refers your company to someone he knows.

<u>Step 2</u>: Your happy customer lets you know that he just referred you to someone.

<u>Step 3</u>: You thank your customer for referring you and ask him when is the best time to contact the referral or if that person plans to contact you.

<u>Step 4</u>: You research the referral. That way, when you contact the referral or the referral contacts you, you have an idea of who the prospect is and what his needs might be.

<u>Step 5</u>: When the referral contacts you or when you contact the referral, schedule an appointment. (Immediately, start your Qualifying process with the referral, asking questions, taking notes, etc.)

<u>Step 6</u>: Provide professional feedback to your customer. Get back with the customer who referred you the work, and let him know how your meeting went. Thank him again for the referral.

About the Author

Justin Jones

Justin C. Jones is a general, roofing, and plumbing contractor. He is a published author of Every Contractors Selling Handbook: How To Round Up Prospects, Build Value, and Get Referrals. Justin is a public speaker who provides valuable insight through Breakout Sessions on Selling and Leadership as a contractor. He speaks to multiple associations and contractors organizations.

Justin owns Heavenly Foundations, where he uses his multiple licenses and extensive contracting expertise to help renovate homes and beautify communities. Justin also operates Contractors Networking, where contractors of various trades can meet up, learn, network and build valuable relationships within the field to help grow each other's businesses and improve the construction industry.

To connect and read Justin's educational sales, leadership and marketing articles and tips, visit http://ContractorsNetworking.com.

Get found using our exclusive Contractors Directory: http://contractorsnetworking.com/signuplanding.aspx

www.ingramcontent.com/pod-product-compliance
Lightning Source LLC
Chambersburg PA
CBHW060641210326
41520CB00010B/1696